And Then There Were Grandchildren

And Then There Were Grandchildren

A Second Generation of Blessing

SHIRLEY BIGGERSTAFF WRIGHT

Foreword by
Larry Minnix

Illustrations by
D. Kenneth Wright

RESOURCE *Publications* · Eugene, Oregon

AND THEN THERE WERE GRANDCHILDREN
A Second Generation of Blessing

Copyright © 2024 Shirley Biggerstaff Wright. All rights reserved. Except for brief quotations in critical publications or review, no part of this book may be reproduced in any manner without prior written permission from the publisher. Write: Permissions, Wipf and Stock Publishers, 199 W. 8th Ave. Suite E, Eugene, OR 97401.

Resource Publications
An Imprint of Wipf and Stock Publishers
199 W. 8th Ave., Suite 3
Eugene, OR 97401

www.wipfandstock.com

PAPERBACK ISBN: 979-8-3852-1732-8
HARDCOVER ISBN: 979-8-3852-1733-5
EBOOK ISBN: 979-8-3852-1734-2

To My Grandchildren

Layers

Long years ago,
I became a daughter,
Much later than that
A wife and a mother.

But now I've become a grandmother,
The crowning glory of my life,
Like whipped cream on top of a sundae,
An added layer of delight.

Contents

Foreword by Larry Minnix xi
Introduction xiii

Joined Our Line 1
Ollie 3
Guy 5
Selma 8
Lily 10
Carl 12
Lucy 14
George 16
Cora 18
Oscar 20
Mamie 22
Albert 24
Inez 26
James 28
Tom 30
Rebecca 32
Poor Jim 35
Harvey 37
Shirley 39
Ken 41
That Great Beyond 43
Serendipity 44
Deliberations 45

Contents

Recycle 46
Duty and Pleasure 47
Child of Blessing 48
Lost Sophistication 49
Multi-tasking 50
Lessons 51
The Flying Chair 53
Conspiracy Theory 54
Legacy 55
The Dress of the Light Blue Hue 57
Changing Vocabulary 59
Routine Saturday 60
At Animal Kingdom 63
A Monopoly 64
Blessing Times Three 65
Called Out 66
Signatures 67
Pictures 68
Treasures 69
Macaroni and Egg Cartons 71
Training the Dog 72
Bonus 73
Fence Posts and Dough Bowls 75
Rocking Chairs 77
Explorers 79
Good for the Soul 80
Nectar of the Gods 83
Traditions 84
Stand Strong 87
Mirror 89
Again Next Year 91
Miles 93
Teachable Moment 95
Blow-Up Castles That Swallow Little Girls 97
Front of the Fire 99
Joy 101

Droolies 103
A Tear or Two 105
Orange Push-Ups 107
Cows 109
Old Chair 111
Heartbreak for Little Kids 113
Hide-and-Seek 115
Good Luck to You 117
Reciprocate 118
Picture Window 119
Oh, the Joy 120
Mother of Mary 121
Salvation 122

Foreword

SHIRLEY WRIGHT HAS A muse on her shoulder. I don't know the name of the muse, but it is older and exhibits all the inevitabilities of the aging process. Picture a grandparent-looking muse. Let's call it "Grandmuse" for the sake of simplicity. In this book of poetry, Grandmuse whispers to Shirley the wit, wisdom, and pathos of a sage—that's "age" with an "s" in front. Grandmuse reflects a twist of Mark Twain with a dash of Flannery O'Conner painted onto our imagination's canvas with the paintbrush of Grandma Moses. You can almost see, hear, and taste the authentic experience of grandparenting through Shirley's poetry—biscuits browning in the oven, the mouth-watering flavor of fresh-churned ice cream.

Grandmuse guides Shirley to recall family "characters," the multi-generation of often eccentric kinfolk that we all have. Laugh and cry as these folks who exhibit the ambiance of small town/rural America come alive from the page and make their way into our imaginations.

For Ken and Shirley, grandparenting is a sacred calling, a ministry. Grandmuse helps Shirley and Ken to locate themselves along the generational line and then to provide lasting recollections to be passed on to future generations as surely as the gene pool conveys traits and tendencies. Poetry is a gift to us that permits our imaginations to conjure up often buried experience that takes us from the near-forgotten to permanent family lore and legacy, the fodder for every family reunion and event. These stories we never tire of hearing even as we watch the youngsters roll their eyes as they are told repeatedly until such time as it is their turn to pass them on. Great poetry helps us to do precisely that—to tell the stories and thereby to preserve them. Grandmuse has inspired a delightful picture of grandparenting through Shirley's artistic talent as a poet. *And Then There Were Grandchildren* is a must read for all "grands" who want to be inspired to fulfill the most important role of their lives should they be fortunate enough to live long and be blessed with grandchildren.

—The Reverend Larry Minnix
Retired Minister, United Methodist Church
Former CEO Wesley Woods, Comprehensive Senior Adult
   Services, Atlanta, GA
Former CEO LeadingAge, Senior Adult Advocacy,
   Washington, D.C.

Introduction

Sometimes—especially as Thanksgiving rolls around—thoughts turn to things for which to be grateful. At times, we even begin to try compiling lists, exhaustive lists, which, of course, is wholly impossible. God, after all, blesses us in so many ways as to make lists escape all our efforts.

When undertaken, however, lists often begin with family. Ken and I, a cup of coffee for each of us, often sit on the side porch, and begin recounting stories we've told a thousand times or more. There's the story of Cora, community doctor, passing her pipe, with leaves from her best medicine plant crushed inside, to a toothache patient. Then there's Albert sitting on a bench in Union, part of the "United Nations." On the Holland side, there's Guy cutting apple peels in one continuous strand, then Ollie cooking them into the world's best pie, or the Biggerstaff side, Lily making strawberry Jell-O topped with cream from milking the cow that very morning. With a second cup of coffee, we might recall a typical Saturday of Ken with his daddy, Jim, or my learning to cook and to sew at the elbow of my mother, Inez.

Moving ahead, our gratitude lists always include the joy of finding one another and doing the foolish thing of getting married while still in college, having very little money but never really feeling impoverished. Then the joy continues—three beautiful children, watching them grow up, find the loves of their own lives. From these marriages have come blessings we will never take for granted—our second generation of blessings—all *twelve* of them. We are so happy to be grandparents, happy for the good times

INTRODUCTION

we've experienced through the years, happy to anticipate good times in the future. There's nothing like having grandchildren to inspire writing—in this case poems. Grab your own cup of coffee, read poems about grandparenting, and enjoy your own memories of grandparents and grandparenting.

Joined Our Line

My side, maternal,
There's Ollie Mae and Guy,
My side, paternal,
There's Lily and Carl.

His side, maternal,
There's Cora and Oscar,
His side, paternal,
There's Mamie and Albert.

My side, maternal,
There's Inez,
My side, paternal,
There's James, and later, Tom.

His side, maternal,
There's Rebecca,
His side paternal,
There's Jim, and later, Harvey.

Then, of course, there's Granddaddy and me,
Shirley and Ken,
More than fifty years and going strong,
Heightened joy when your parents were born.

Then there's you,
Wonderful you, and I can say—Granddaddy too—
That we're glad you came,
Joined our line.

Ollie

She tended the home fires
Careful as could be,
Fresh pans of biscuits
Morning and night, you see.

And her apple pies
Were a joy and delight
And I vowed to practice
Her recipe 'til I got it right.

I'd scream and yell unless
She be the one held my head under water,
For she could do it as none other,
Water, shampoo with never a splatter.

She was my hero,
And I remember when
She died a part of me died too,
Me at tender age of ten.

It's a good thing that I got
Part of her name,
My daughter handed it to her daughter,
So, in name, we're the same.

Now to Lily Mae,
If to you, I can only be,
What Ollie Mae
Was for me!

Guy

He built houses
Just he and a lone
Helper, bottom to top,
Foundation to roof.

Some of those houses
Stand to this day,
And families living there praise him,
His being a testament to hard work.

I was never witness to
All that work—only heard
Stories about it—what amazed me
Was something different altogether.

He'd come home,
Sit in his rocking chair
His fifteen-inch black-and-white
Just a few feet in front of him.

He'd tune up Perry Como
And tease us that it was
Perry Come-Over, then he'd
Laugh his delight at all our objections.

Meanwhile he'd gather
His pocket knife and apples
From the tree in the pasture
Back of the house.

He'd cut rings
Of peelings, beginning to end,
One long strip, and I declared
Never to have seen such a feat!

And so I pledged
That I'd practice and practice,
And when I was good and grown,
I'd be just like him.

Not a bad aspiration after all.

Selma

We—
our family—the brunt of many jokes
About a family tree
With no branches,

We
Sit and calmly explain
My dad, an early death,
Then a new dad, stepdad to be completely clear.

Grandmother—
Mom's mom—also an
Early death, so Grandpa
Marries Selma, Stepdad's sister.

And that's when
You became not only
Aunt Selma, but technically
Also our grandmother.

Children
Born to me then?
Well for them, you are
Granny Aunt Selma!

Lily

Her adult children
Living lives of their own
'cept for my dad
Drowned years ago,
Dread loneliness of grief.

She lived on a dirt road
Cut off from the main
Of civilization by a highway
And the D.O.T. paid far
Too little for her farmland,
'specially for the growing
Loneliness it added.

We prided ourselves
On our infrequent visits,
Our chattering about our lives,
Those of her great-grandchildren.
She was a quiet soul, had always been,
But when we prepared
To leave she could always
Be heard to say,
"You'uns come back, and
Don't wait so long!"

Carl

Most times you could barely
Know he was in the room,
Seems like his responses
Were more like grunts
Than real words.

He sat with us on
The front porch
Smoking his cigarettes despite
Already diagnosed with emphysema,
Not only from the vile weed
But the puffs of cotton
Pervading the air in the mill
Where he worked faithfully
To support his family.

I can't remember
A single thing he said
What I remember is his
Devotion to Lily beginning to end,
And the way he'd get in
His black '46 Ford,
List in hand and he'd return
From the country store
With some bottles of Pepsi
And boxes of Jell-O,
Whatever she needed
To bring us joy.

Lucy

Please hear it, set the record straight,
Any dear woman, who's the mother of eight,
Most certainly a saint, deserves our accolades.

When I knew her, they were all gone,
Grown, married, families of their own,
What I remember is how she loved the phone.

Friend on the other end, she'd talk through the crossword,
The endeavor—half of her day? No, maybe only a third!
Today we might call her the TV Guide nerd.

Loved fried eggs only on the right kind of plate,
Blue Willow for her, runny eggs on white she certainly did hate,
A phobia? A simple quirk? It's difficult to rate.

Most important thing I remember 'bout her—her love for me and my brother,
Grandchildren just like all of the others,
Nothing called step in her vocabulary. She became our third grandmother.

George

He must've been patient, the father of eight,
Stood side by side with his lifelong mate.

Lived in the village, worked hard at the mill,
Hard times, he must've had his fill.

Like Lucy's giving birth, one twin dead,
Or the fire taking the little they had.

But to George it never once occurred
Talk about pain, said never a word.

One of his loves 'sides Lucy, rest of the family,
His walnut tree, picked fruit so patiently,

'til Christmas at hand, Lucy was known to bake,
The time-honored, world's best walnut cake!

Cora

Cora, a name to borrow
For your great, great-granddaughter,
With you gone, it lives for the morrow.

But live, live, as well,
Are stories they tell
Of time long past, your place to fill.

You tended fields, carried your weight in cotton
Sprung forth from burs in the late of autumn,
Seven children you raised, so not soon forgotten.

You had the time-honored opportunity
To be recognized as the country doctor,
Served them all—the whole community.

Not from books, no formal education,
You taught yourself 'bout trees, plants, and seeds,
What herbs brought healing in every situation.

With toothaches, from miles around they came
Seeking your pipe filled with leaves plucked
From the plant your garden's fame.

Someone suggested you use the name
For a daughter, one or two down the line,
But you protested—just the plant—your sweet Mary Jane.

Oscar

Your name—it's borrowed too,
There we find it sprung anew,
A great, great grandson who follows you.

There you were, barely five-feet-two,
So hard it must have been
To find, for your foot a size six shoe.

A tenant farmer knew your time in dirt,
But Saturday for trips to town or Sundays to go to church,
You'd don your suit, not overalls and flannel shirt.

Maybe there was a time, a bumper crop,
But somehow you bought, not a wagon,
But a surrey with fringe on the top.

Mamie

Her name was Mamie,
And it's clear, she looks so dainty.

A carefully-pressed dress, no matter the weather,
She made sachets, filled the air with heather.

She grew roses along with rose-grower friends,
Friendships like theirs, never fences to mend.

Among them a long, long-standing tradition,
Cover of night, steal a cutting, but never—never ask for permission.

Whatever the things in her day's tasks,
She'd tune up *Love of Life* with its beloved cast.

We treasure thoughts of this Southern lady and the life she chose,
But did I forget to say how much she loved her Tube Rose?

Albert

His real name was Albert,
But they all called him Rabbit,
Grew up in Union,
Stayed there his whole life,
'cept for time he served his country,
A merchant marine.

Remembered as a fair and honest worker,
Supervising on the mill hill,
For thirty-plus years
He served his time,
Impossible for a guy like him
To sit down, while away the hours,
So he delivered flowers
For his son, florist in town.

Three fender-benders later
They took his keys,
Maybe that's when he did
His life's best work,
Gathering with friends
Under giant oaks,
Four benches set in a square
They dubbed it the United Nations,
And together they solved
The problems of the world.

Inez

Did God will that early
She sit down to her mother's old Singer,
Or that she learn to love
Feel of fabric 'tween her fingers,
Or that she stand in awe the magic
How flat, useless fibers,
A pattern, some thread
Could weave something useful,
How her creation could
Bring others joy and delight?

Did God will that
She learn to love dirt also 'tween her fingers,
That she always see the miracle
Of seeds, with earth, water,
And tender, loving care would sprout tiny leaves,
Then grow and grow 'til we need transplant
Them, bigger and bigger pots,
Finally maturing into something
So beautiful that people would stop,
Pay their money and take them home?

Did God will that these two things
She so dearly loved,
Be not just hobbies, but
Ways she provide for us,
Still staying at home?

James

Why couldn't I have known you?
I ask that nearly every day,
Perhaps I shouldn't question decisions
You made, but really couldn't you stay?

Stay home that weekend,
We might have been little, my brother and me,
But couldn't you have taken us shopping
Mother's Day gifts her to please?

Or if money were tight as surely it was,
Maybe you simply could've traced little hands
On paper folded in half, inscribed
Words, "Love you more—more than anyone can."

But sixty-nine years and I'm still saying,
Wish you'd learned safety—float, swim, float—
The decisions we make with scarcely a thought,
Wish you'd donned a jacket 'fore you got in the boat!

Tom

Had eyes for the same redhead,
Tom and James, but still they were friends,
We're not sure how it all played out, what led
To James'—not Tom's decision—to ask for her hand.

Tom—he moved on with his life,
Friends still with James, no fences to mend,
His marriage? There always was strife,
Was it this or other sadness caused his back to bend?

Fast forward a few more years,
The redhead, two dark-haired little ones,
Make James' life complete—no worries, no fears,
But an ill-fated accident made all that to end.

Two years later Tom asked the question, "Could I be bold, brave
Enough—Wait! How would if look for him to date
The redhead?" Maybe he'd sit by the grave
Of his lost friend, question the one met a calamitous fate.

Guess he heard "yes" from the great beyond,
'cause he soon began to call at her front door,
But rarely was it just two of them—two kids 'round
You see—so dates most often, not two but four!

The kids always included, it makes sense you see,
The little girl exclaiming, "Guess we married him, didn't we?"

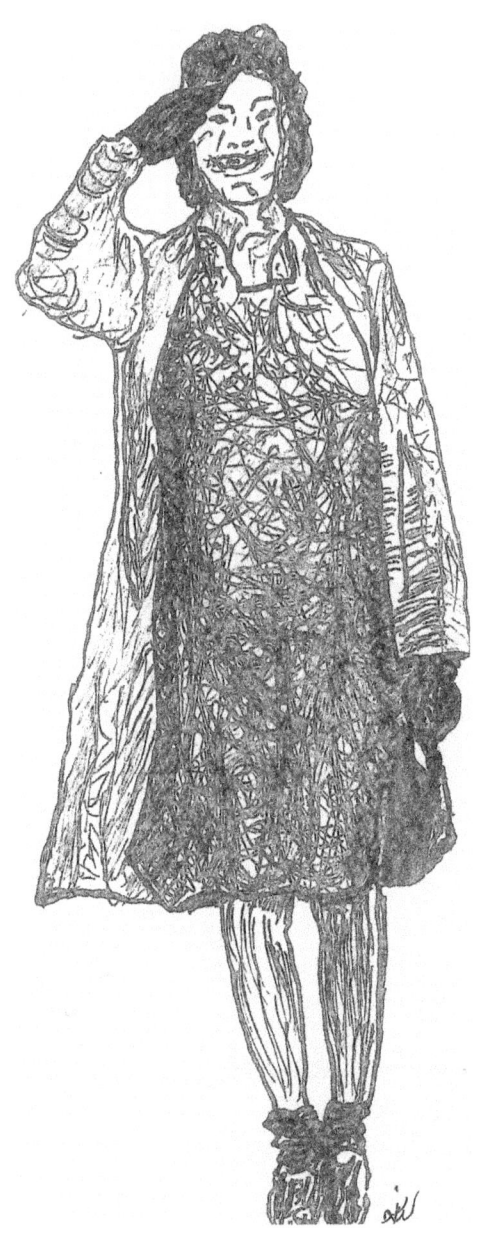

Rebecca

Woman called by many names,
Rebecca the name her mother gave her,
But when she heard Becky she also came.

Still another, to it she would answer,
Best Southern dialect, rules like "Drop the 'a,' add 'er,'"
The name this time, not Becky, but Becker!

She was born the youngest of seven,
The siblings stood up for her, even took her lickins',
For they loved her, from earth clear to heaven.

The youngest at home,
She took care of Mom,
A homebody we'd expect never to roam.

But she met a beau, caught her catch,
She loved him, declared him
Her very best match.

They pledged their troth on their special day,
A short time together,
Before he went away.

Hard times—young couples saying goodbyes
Never knowing when they'd see each other again,
Leaving home she waved from the train with never a sigh.

For days, along with other wives, traveled to the West Coast,
Treasuring each moment they'd have with their men,
And in separate love stories they'd be found to boast.

But finally, it was time for her Jim to ship overseas,
So she headed home with his family to live, praying constant prayers
"Bring him home, Lord, home if you please."

What kept her going, and him much more,
Were the letters they'd write,
Airmail delivery, shore to another shore.

When Rebecca told it—their love story—
Nothing better in life than meeting, getting married,
But then another chapter in all its glory.

That chapter? Well, it's you, of course,
You, their Kenny, their son,
The joy of all joys—you were the source!

Poor Jim

Poor Jim,
That's what they called him,
Not James or simply Jim,
His hometown of Union,
He was always Poor Jim.

Later pictures of him,
When we'd see them, wonder set in,
For nothing about him was incredibly thin,
Guess we'd have had to know him,
Know him back then.

But big man, it seems so right,
'cause he looms large, large in their sight,
Not in measurements, not simply a number,
Instead, he looms large insofar as his character,
And they'll remember him, both now and forever.

The stories? The stories they told?
They were about his heart, heart of pure gold,
They talked of needs that he'd embrace,
Come to aid in every case,
And injustice—wipe it away—find no trace.

Me? Never knew Poor Jim,
Though thankful always for stories of him,
Forever grateful for a different part
Of Poor Jim, how to Kenny—his only son—he taught character,
How to live, how to have a heart.

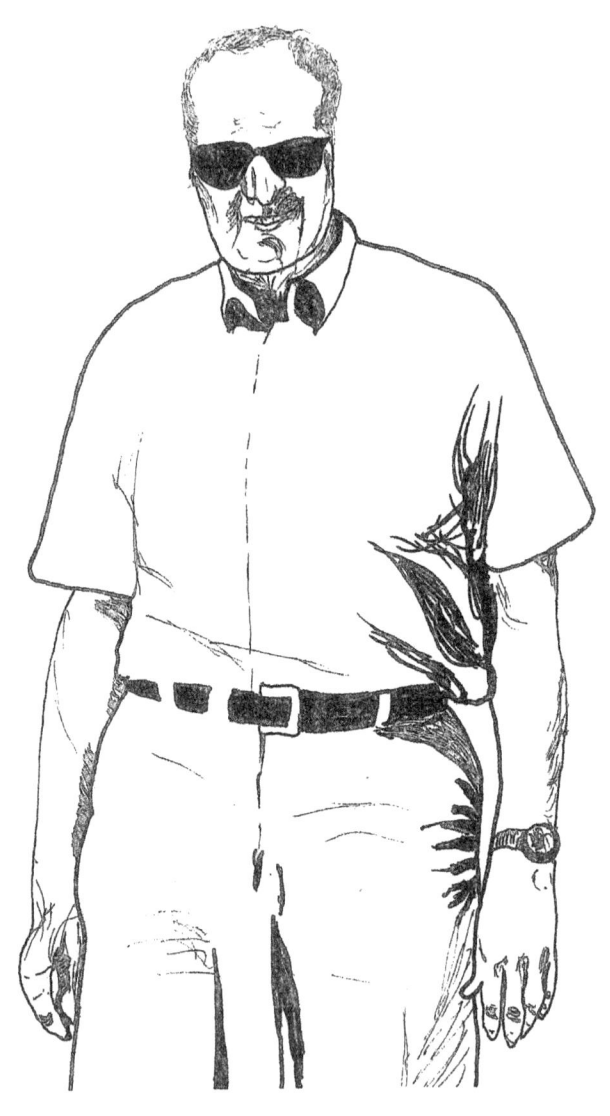

Harvey

A baseball player turned semi-pro,
A salesman, you were in the know,
Sell swimsuits to Eskimos as the saying goes.

Savannah, she held your heart,
Grew up there, got your start,
Jobs? They took you away. With your return, pledged never to part.

Your salesman self, you were known to wander,
Becky's Fashions of Carolina—it was there you met her,
Right sweet nothings in her ear you were found to whisper.

How do we know these things? For others—long before you,
Had come, had been there too,
Promising lives of ease, pledging hearts so true.

Each in his own way charming,
Surprising how vehement her rejecting,
Guess the saying is true, "All a matter of timing."

Moved with you to Savannah, she was born anew,
First real adolescence, we declare it's true,
Apart from older siblings, it's there she grew.

Guess I need say thank you to you,
But need whisper words for him too,
Take over work of caring for mom? A gift out of the blue.

Shirley

Lived, grew up,
Western North Carolina,
Hearing her, you
Know the accent
Never left her.

Mom, Dad, brother,
A small farm,
Few natural distractions,
But never allowed
The word, "bored,"
Developing hobbies, she
Practiced the piano,
Cooked and sewed,

Skills still useful
Today but best
Of her life,
Wasn't back then,
Not in Carolina,
Though good as
Could be, instead,
All the places
Along with you.

Ken—the love
Of her life,
Then, her beloved children,
Their spouses,
And then the
Twelve grandchildren who followed!

Ken

What shall I say,
Say about you?
Only child, loved
By both parents,
But with Dad,
A special bond,
Pledged to be like him
In all you do.

A latch-key kid,
Much time on your
Hands, liked building forts
With other kids, 'til
Their moms called them
In, then riding bike,
To downtown Woodruff,
And shaking hands
With all the merchants,
A real politician.

More time alone,
Any wonder you
Learned love for reading,
Encyclopedias, any book
You could find,
Any wonder today
You surround yourself
Here, there, everywhere,
Shelf after shelf.

James Melvin Wright,
I never knew him,
But glad he
Cloned his heart,
Stuffed it into you,
The love of my life.

That Great Beyond

Who would have dreamed there was something
in that great beyond—
> Beyond diapers and cries
> And the first knowing smile,
> Beyond tottering steps
> And a bike ridden with training wheels,
> And keys for the car handed over with trepidation,
> Beyond "Mom, I love her,"
> And spoken, "I do's."

But I awaken and I am a resident
of that great beyond—
> Diapers and cries
> And the waiting smile,
> Legs rehearsing those tottering steps,
> A bike at Kmart patient for its soon-to-be owner,
> The first date in preparation in the cradle next door,
> Keys for a car still held in imagination,
> Words, "Mom, he is my love," held back for a time,
> And dispersed crowds, later to gather to hear "I do's."

Thank you, God, there is something
in that great beyond
> And thank God
> For child of my child.

Serendipity

When I look into your face—
   A moment of magic,
   A heart full of delight,
   A serendipity beyond compare.

When I look into your face
   I see hope and promise—
   Beyond myself,
   Beyond my child.

And I say to the Creator Almighty,
   "Thank you, God!"

Deliberations

"Shall we choose James or Jordon,"
they wondered with intensity,
"or if she's a girl,
will Cora or Carrie be best?"

On other occasions they
balanced the scales between
Timothy or Thomas
and between Sarah or Suzanne.

But we held our
own special deliberations,
Should we be Grandmother and Grandfather,
or Nanna and Pop?

Would MaMaw and PaPaw
fit our personalities
or Grandma and Grandpa
suit us best?

Then we sat in quiet anticipation
knowing that whatever
you call us will certainly
please us the most.

Recycle

Paper and plastic,
Glass bottles, aluminum cans,
Give them opportunities
To show up once again,
Here and there on grocery shelves.

Names, Cora or Oscar,
Kenneth or Mae,
Once is never enough,
Recycle them,
Other generations to yours.

Duty and Pleasure

Mother hurried about the house
And took care of things,
She cooked and she cleaned and assured
The household was a model of efficiency.

But Grandmother sat down
In a porch swing, a chair nearby,
And watched our imaginings, coming to participate
Whenever given the invitation.

Her job was one my mother envied,
The time to watch—to encourage flights of fantasy,
The ability to say "yes" to most every entreaty
From persuasive child's eyes.

She had the hard job,
While Grandmother had the pleasurable one,
Thank you, thank you, God,
That after doing the hard job, I now have all the pleasure.

Child of Blessing

O Child,
Little Child,
Child of Blessing,
Child of Love,
We hold you
Up to God
Today as we
Have every day,
But today especially
As we lift you up,
We ask for forgiveness
In our lives
And for guidance
That God may
Lead us
In right paths
So that we
May take you
With us
On right paths.
We lift you
Up to God
Today and sprinkle
You with the
Waters of God's
Grace and love.

Lost Sophistication

We cluck and coo
And speak in monosyllables
Long ago abandoned
For language appropriate to age.

We squat on all fours
To provide piggy-back rides,
Quote Dr. Suess and Berenstain Bears
As if Shelley or Byron or Keats.

To what do we attribute
Such lapse
From our usual decorum
And sophistication?

We say it in a single sentence,
"We are grandparents!"

Multi-tasking

Multi-tasking, you say?
Some might describe as
Laundry in the machine
While also cooking lunch,
Others recall
Walking the treadmill
While watching a self-help video,
Some say it's
Helping with homework
While finishing a report for work,
Some describe
Watching the Braves
While also the Falcons and Furman on T.V.,
The latter, of course,
Leaving my head to spin
A thousand different directions.

But me?
My chief multi-tasking event?
Well, it's clear, of course,
It's weeding the flower bed
While also helping you to find worms
To stuff into your coffee-can-worm-bucket.

Lessons

What will I
Teach you
In the days
That we have?

Will I teach
You to ride
A bike or to
Read a book?

Will I teach
You to hit
A ball or to
Swim a lap?

Who can say?
Only time will tell,
Open its discoveries
To the two of us.

But regardless of these,
Ah, that I
Could teach you to love life,
To live it to the fullest.

The Flying Chair

Ugly and brown,
Taking up half the room,
The décor it was designed to fit?
Well, surely there was none.

Arms wide with flaps
That opened to swallow
The remote, glasses,
A snack or two,
Every month, two, or four,
A high recommendation
To do deep cleaning,
See what grows there.

But mornings or evenings,
For watching T.V.
We knew where to look,
Exactly where you would be.

For there with Granddaddy,
Wings of the old worn recliner,
You even named it,
Called it the Flying Chair!

Conspiracy Theory

Grandparents must forge their own language,
It's in the rule book, you see,
And it must be shared in secret with the generation
Once removed from them, guarding every so carefully
That it never pass into the hands of the enemy—
The generation in between.

Just take, for example, the code
That Grandpa shared with my brother and with me—
Each weekly shopping trip he announced his intention
To buy dog biscuits, and the three of us disappeared
Into the cave of the candy counter at the five-and-dime
Where toasty, crunchy, coconut morsels satiated us
Much like "biscuits" for our mongrel dog.

We were sure Mom was none the wiser,
It was a great conspiracy, you see,
And I can hardly wait to forge
A new conspiracy between you and me.

Legacy

There are some sorts of things,
Some good and some bad,
They pass from one generation
To another, skipping one in between.

And so it sets me to wondering,
What will be my legacy to you?
Certainly not my sometimes moodiness
Nor my patience that wears too thin.

Oh, that I could
Pass to you instead,
Music always in my heart,
And joy deep within my soul!

The Dress of the Light Blue Hue

It was a dress of a light blue hue,
Puffy sleeves, a little round collar
With white, tatted lace sewn on the edges.

Not bought at a store,
Not a fancy boutique,
Rather smocked by Grandmother, sewn by Mother.

When granddaughters were born,
Thought it her duty to pleat, then stitch,
Then pass to Mother for sewing.

So she pleated for me, that light blue swatch,
Then fashioned her geometrics
In pink, blue, and white.

I thought that never had I been
Prettier than I was then,
In that dress of a light blue hue.

Then when you, the first
Came along, I felt it incumbent on me
To learn to pleat and stitch the swatches, then sew the dresses.

Of Christmas plaids, or ones of the light blue hue,
Stitched with angels for
What had become the three of you.

Time moved on, never missing a year,
Of pleating, smocking and sewing,
But wait, this year there are six of you!

What shall I do, do this year,
No longer three girls to dress
In a light blue hue?

Rather three boys join in,
So I must plan ahead,
Green and red plaid, that's what it will be.

Jumpers for girls, rompers for boys,
White-pleated panels sewn in,
Each smocked with different toys.

So that's what can come
From a dress of a light blue hue
Smocked by Grandmother, then sewn by Mother.

Changing Vocabulary

"No," becomes "Yes,"
"You've got to be more careful,"
Becomes, "That's okay,"
Study hard," becomes
"Have lots of fun,"
"Eat your vegetables,"
Becomes "Here's your dessert,"
"You can't have that,"
Becomes "Grandma will get it for you!"

Ah, how language changes
As one moves from parenting to grandparenting!

Routine Saturday

Routine
Saturday, get up,
Dressed, breakfast of
Bacon-wrapped steak with
Buttered toast, then
Clean the house,
Off to town,
Lunch Townhouse Café.

Off to the
Service station, stand
One side of
The street with
Dad talking to
Everyone he meets,
And son playing
In the alley
His own little
Games, 'til time
For afternoon matinee,
A delightful cartoon,
Then action-packed Western.
Then time to
Position themselves on
The other side
Of the street,
Dad carries on
Conversation with shoppers
There, for he
Knows them all,

Meanwhile, the son
clutches his nickel
Given by Dad,
'til he spends
It for a
Cone of vanilla
The Anthony Pharmacy.

Pick up Mom,
Off to the
Beloved Do Drive-in
For French fries
And hot dogs,
Home they tune
Up the T.V.
Where they watch
Gunsmoke, Paladin, Harrigan.

Routine, but every
Saturday, especially for
Time with dad…
Special.

At Animal Kingdom

Her eyes light up,
And her mouth forms
A perfect circle
While her tiny hands
Move an adult head
In the direction
She wants it to go,
And she says,
"You see it?"
"You see it, MaMaw?"
"You see 'ose an'mals?"

Now that's a wonder!

A Monopoly

Sometimes, it's true, you see
That children, regarding ghosts and spirits, claim a monopoly.

No sooner had we moved in
Than our three claimed to hear a voice so thin.

And they even professed to see her,
A fragile old woman floating as if on air.

Busy, always busy, my husband and I,
Were dismissive of these reports, I won't lie.

That is, until a new generation came along
And hearing the stories their fears were strong.

Terrified they were at the very thought
Of spending nights with us, other grandparent lodging they sought.

We reprimanded our children as if they were two or three,
Implanting fear about our old house, an insult to husband and me.

But now times are slower, and I am free
To poke and prod for any spirit there may be.

Sometimes I cherish thoughts of conversation with that voice so thin,
Maybe I'll ask her if later I might move in . . .

As a spirit floating on air,
Greeting new children at the top of the stair.

Blessing Times Three

If grandparents could spoil a child,
Then hopelessly spoiled I would be,
For life dealt me early misfortune
My dad gone long before I was three.

But God looked down and touched us,
And gently salved our grief,
A new daddy, a new set of grandparents—
Blessings—blessings times three.

"I turned out not so badly," I declare
As I look in my mirror, see the person I know me to be
So I shall never worry
About spoiling grandchildren given to me,

For I had three sets of grandparents,
Spoiling-potential times three!

Called Out

I remember times
when you would visit,
I was very calm, demure,
as I finished the meal
for all who were there.

The dishes in the sink,
food in the fridge, time
to turn attention to you,
Come on. Let the games begin,
most often, chase, running
circular paths through den,
kitchen and hall.

But me, the older, more experienced one,
knew how to fake you out,
running a different direction
than you were expecting,
then shouting "Boo!" to your face,
but parents, they certainly weren't happy.

For them, time to calm the kids,
make them ready for bed,
So that's when I hit a new state of humiliation,
called out not by a teacher, a parent,
or elder, called out instead
by my very own daughter!

Signatures

Grandmothers leave their signatures
Upon the lives of the grandchildren,
Like apple pies that will be points of comparison
For all apple pies in their future
Or like gestures of love
Through a beautiful dress made for a special occasion.

Grandfathers leave their signature in other ways,
In lessons taught about importance of applying brakes
On the car made together,
When fast approaching the neighbor's Cadillac
Parked innocently alongside the street,
Sometimes in aerodynamic principles
Shared while whittling the magical, first soap-box racer.

The signatures are indelible,
They help shape us into the persons that we are
And the persons we will be
When we are grandparents.

Pictures

There are pictures carved
As deeply in my mind
As those forged in rock
On the face of Stone Mountain.

That of Grandpa Holland's peeling apples for me,
One long, continuous strand of residue coming from his hand,
Grandma Holland's lathering my head and pouring water
Ever so gently so not even a droplet escaped to my eyes.

One of Grandpa Biggerstaff's shuffling us to his tired, old car
For trips to the country store where clutched nickels exchanged for treats,
And Grandma Biggerstaff's topping heavenly strawberry Jell-O
With cream whipped from her cow milked that morning.

I cannot so easily reproduce these
Masterpieces and give them all to you,
But we can begin our own special journey that
Will etch itself into pictures all your own.

Treasures

When my parents died,
They left behind the treasures
Of my children's
Childhood.

There was the Fisher-Price farm,
The peg bench with the
Now too-loose pegs and the bedraggled
Doll.

And so I began that day
To collect the necessities
For a new generation of
Grandchildren.

A chest full of blocks,
A giraffe puzzle,
An ensemble of dolls and another of
Bears.

I supply the basics,
They supply the imagination and
From the two will come my grandchildren's
Treasures.

Macaroni and Egg Cartons

Treasures clutched in little hands
And hidden behind the backs of their makers,
Await an eager grandmother
Feigning more surprise than is honest,
Through one set of eyes there are only Dixie cups
With thimbles-full of dirt,
And spindly, pink petunias,
Or there are simple egg cartons,
Bedecked with macaroni
And sprayed a sparkly gold,
But in a grandmother's eyes
They are the gardens *par excellence*
That her little one intends,
Or the jewelry chests for
The finest of her jewelry.

Training the Dog

Four grandchildren
From my daughter's home,
A big space, then another
Came along.

After that
No need for outside entertainment,
For she was worth more than any dollars we might
Have spent.

I remember
The very day sitting with the five
Over dinner when with laughter the four
Come alive.

I responded,
Hearing Little One's request, I had given her seconds of bread,
Heard, "Good job, MaMaw!" funniest words ever
She'd said.

The reason?
Laughs so huge they dissolved into sobs?
Those words she'd learned as they trained
The dog!

Bonus

The regular paycheck,
A joy, a delight,
Then there's that Christmas bonus
One to never quite anticipate,
Certainly to never take for granted.

The bonus came early that year,
Actually two of them,
Not Christmastime at all,
Rather my birthday,
And through that wedding,
Two bonus grandchildren.

Fence Posts and Dough Bowls

Our grandfathers mended fence posts,
Plowed gardens, and fed the livestock,
Our grandmothers kneaded bread,
Fried fat back, rocked babies in the cool of the porch.

Their hands held hammers
And mules' reigns, and garden hoes,
They knew the touch of wooden dough bowls,
And iron pans, and warm dirt nurturing flower gardens.

Be we, dear man,
What about us?
We know little about hammers and garden hoes,
Iron pans and successful gardening in the warm dirt.

Should we be flies on the wall
For future conversations and photo-swap sessions
Among our kin, what pictures will
Warm their hearts as they tell stories of us?

Rocking Chairs

Tall-backed oak ones,
Carved deeply at a master's touch,
Small sewing ones minus arms
To get in the way,
Sturdy, rustic ones painted an ugly green
And placed on the front porch,
The wood of some stained black
With cushioned seats of Naugahyde,
Delicate white wicker ones
Just begging for a nursery—
It matters not the materials,
It matters not their design,

The two were made to go together—
Grandparents and rocking chairs.

Explorers

They dream of new worlds,
And grandparents at their behest
Launch them in their excursions where
Bountiful treasures greet them in the quest.

Doorways open—not passages to India
Or to farthest places underneath the sun—
But on stairways to Grandma's attic, explorers
They become, Columbus or Magellan.

Good for the Soul

Time to tell the truth,
Set the record straight,
After all, don't they say
Confession is good for the soul?

Well, time marches on,
And I'm getting old,
So I truly need something,
Anything good for the soul.

No matter what you've thought
Your assessment of yourselves matched to your elders,
The old and the very old, are not perfect,
And never have been.

I want to point you to them,
Sometimes they were clever
We're still hearing the stories unexpected moments
'bout some of their escapades.

Other times, though, caught in the act,
Being somewhere other than
Where they should have been, or playing
Ferris Bueller, the joy of skipping school.

Oh, wait a minute, I digress.
Maybe we could talk about Granddaddy next,
But not really my story to tell, and maybe he
Was just a good and perfect kid, a single child.

But me, now that's another story,
After all, an older brother,
Potential for leading me astray,
I remember the time, just like it was today.

We borrowed cigarettes,
Kitchen drawer, right-hand side,
Found our secret hiding spot,
Other side of the tracks.

There we lighted up
And all was well,
Guess Daddy never counted his cigarettes
Or thought he'd smoked far more than he really had.
Least we didn't set anything on fire,
Or catch an immediate fit of lung disease,
But there, I've said, it,
Sat in the confessional booth with you.

What? What was the deterrent to another adventure
Such as this? Well there was a slight oversight,
On our part—poison ivy vines all around,
Treatment being shots every day for a week!

So now my soul? It feels much better!

Nectar of the Gods

In my day it happened like this—
Grandpa whisked us away to the ice plant
While Grandma finished the dishes from supper,
And when we returned, we watched the magical
Blend of ice and salt, ice and salt
That cradled a center of milk, eggs, and sugar,
One grandchild and then another perched atop the dutiful machine,
While the adults took turns cranking, each dreading being
The last who would labor over the tortuous handle,
When the once-liquid contents yielded to the
Frozen nectar of the gods.

But today it happens like this—
Having passed the hospital's course,
"Correct Installation of Car Safety Seats,"
We harness and hook each little device,
And then coax the little ones in,
Promising them surprises they can only begin to imagine,
We leave our well-manicured neighborhood
For the lure of a spit-polished, yuppy establishment
Where a yawning teenager delights us and the grandchildren
By serving up cones filled with the frozen nectar of the gods.

Traditions

Every family has them,
Especially for holiday times,
Although we can't always remember
Just when they were born.

Turkey for Thanksgiving,
Christmas, a ham in the stove,
For breakfast eggs
Topping the can
Of corned beef hash,
Dinner for both occasions
Something easy you see,
Make a big bowl of oyster stew,
And desserts, we must have them
Served in abundance,
So nut cake from the
Wright side of the family,
Slices served alongside of ambrosia,
Passed on to us from my own mother,
Fresh apple cake with warm brown sugar sauce.

So, that's it, the things we eat,
But then there are the things we do with our time,
One year, we don't remember when,
Granddaddy invented the idea for Christmas,
A Wright Family talent show,
I admit, I was skeptical at the time,
Of just what all of you would think,
Whether you'd pull through,
Solos, magic tricks, form groups

Like The Slippery Biscuits,
Now I'm only left to wonder
When the talent scout will show up

Only to discover you.

Stand Strong

I started sewing so long ago,
Seems like I've always sewn,
My toy Singer clamped
To Mother's sewing table,
Our machines clanging along
In happy rhythms together.

Doll clothes, the quilt with the chain stitch,
Blouses for myself, all out of scraps
Mother's customers left for us,
With a new generation I sewed costumes,
Clowns, Batman and Robin, tiny dresses,
Then prom gowns and bridesmaids' attire.

Another generation I smocked and sewed,
Christmas plaids with geometric designs,
Angel patterns, snowflakes, and toys—
Airplanes, trucks and trains.

Energy for sewing, I must admit,
Sometimes it comes and sometimes it goes,
One of my great joys are times I receive pleas
For a dress to ready you for a book report.

And so we researched Ruby Bridges,
Copied the fabric and pattern near as we could
And there you stood,
Beautiful in your dress.

And you talked about her,
The little girl in the midst of strife and pain,
Wearing a cute dress and being strong.
May that dress remind you, no matter what comes your way…

To stand strong.

Mirror

When I look into my mirror,
I cannot deny the midriff bulges
Come to replace the
Once slender, firm figure of my youth.

When I look into my mirror,
I cannot deny the wisps
Of gray, nor crow's feet and lines
About my eyes and mouth.

And when I look to my world
For affirmation, I hear instead
Assumptions that my life
Is now all but over.

But when I look into
The mirrors of my grandchildren's eyes,
I have all the affirmation
That I could ever need.

When I look into
The mirrors of my grandchildren's eyes,
I see the message
Spelled out bold and clear,

"Thank you for just being you!
We love you just the way you are!"

Again Next Year

I count the literal cost.

Raised beds times two,
Two hundred dollars,
Fill dirt for both,
Seventy dollars or more.

Then I count wear and tear on myself.

Body aches and pains
From all the lifting,
Hours spent in the hot sun
With near heat exhaustion.

I look at the sparsely-developing fruit.

I can only conclude,
That it's not worth it,
Not worth it in the actual economy,
Not worth it in bodily aches and pains.

But then you come for a visit.

As luck would have it,
It's harvest time,
And I hold you up to reach
The fruit at the tips of tall stems.

And I breath in your response.

Your joy cannot be contained
As you pluck the luscious fruit,
Five—that's all there is,
But it's more than enough!

Guess I'll be planting again next year!

Miles

We were miles
Along our journey,
Granddaddy and me.

Thought we'd read
Past the chapters of welcoming
New little ones to the family.

But Granddaddy chided them,
Said to our three, "Always thought,
I'd be Granddaddy to at least twelve!"

So many miles along the journey,
With the number still stuck, stuck at eleven,
The chiding by this time almost gone quiet.

But then they came with the
Surprising announcement,
And then, there was . . .

Miles.

Teachable Moment

They come in the strangest of times
And in the strangest of ways,
And, no doubt shop owners,
And restaurant workers of every kind
Sometimes cringe when they see us come in,
Grandparents, parents galore,
And three little ones 'neath the age of four,
Never thinking for a moment
'bout the teachable moment that we have in store.

We consider ourselves lucky
To make it through serving lines,
Plates served, high chairs in tow,
Giving thanks for even a few peaceful
Moments to eat, but after the meal's
Been inhaled by the three,
Time to play, to run 'round the room.

So the two older ones with boundless energy,
Circle our chairs, running faster and faster,
Chanting over and over again,
"Granddaddy, Granddaddy, Granddaddy!"
And in due time, the youngest, barely one,
Repeats the pattern, chimes your name,
"Granddaddy, Granddaddy, Granddaddy,"
We smiled, lifted words of praise,
Who would have thought?
Who could have known, a teachable moment
Right there in Stew-n-Que,
For up until then for her you'd been KeKe!

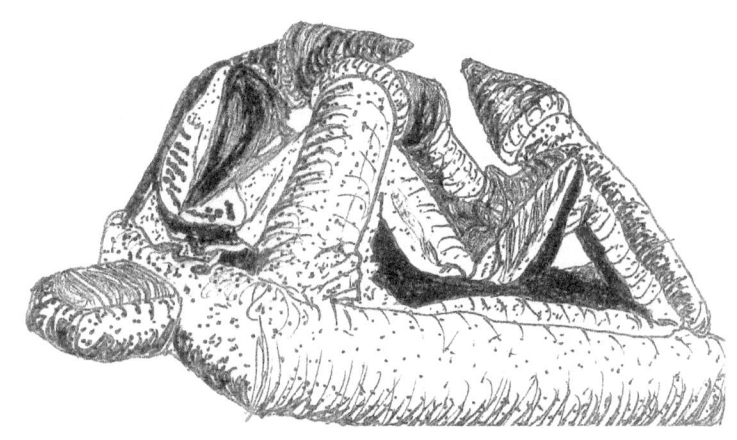

Blow-Up Castles That Swallow Little Girls

We're a litigious society,
So, really, truly there
Must be someone to blame.

The City of Lula?
Planners of the fall festival?
Owners of the rented equipment?

They simply must pay,
Provide lifetime therapy for the little girl
Swallowed by the castle.

A burst of wind
Catching the tethers,
Then folding her in.

So all of you argue
There's no predicting that,
The factors that led to her trauma.

But I'm here to tell you
Something simply must be done
For I'm the grandmother,

Whose blow-up mattress
Threatens to swallow little girls!

Front of the Fire

There you were
Front of the fire you'd made,
Reminding me ever so much
Of your dad,
Always our chief fire-maker,
And thankful we were for the skill he honed,
For always first up and out of the tent,
He warmed the air so then
Comfortable for me to cook.

Gathering around the perfected blaze,
Spears in hand, we load our treats,
And that's when you decided,
Let the stories begin.

And you each shared thoughts about
Your early memories, especially
Houses we lived in when
You came to visit.
Along with marshmallows and chocolate,
Joy spilled over your face
As you recalled times with cousins,
House after house, wherever we lived.

Joy

Outfits made,
You all dressed in them,
Time to haul you
To photographer's studio
With deep hopes for perfect
Smiles spread across each face.

Wonder and delight,
When results come in,
Expressions uniquely you.

Mouth formed into a perfect round "O,"
You could have convinced anyone around
You were lost in strains of
"Joy to the World," and so,
Every year on my Christmas mantle,
There you are in my JOY frame.

Droolies

Droolies—most times altogether
Unseemly, unspoken discomfort
From those who observe.

But with you,
Altogether different,
There you were,
Oldest of your family,
With a picture to capture
Each and every accomplishment.

But this day,
Not flipping over,
Not crawling,
Nor sitting up,
Not the fact that
You looked cute
Sporting that adorable
Blue toile suit.

Simply the little
Droplet, the drooly
Sitting on your chin.

A Tear or Two

It's not in us,
Not in grandparents
To ever want to see sadness
In the face of a grandchild.

Not in us to be witnesses
To tears welling up in eyes
Without trying to fix it,
Whatever the hurt.

Well, maybe there's a single
Exception to the rule,
There being a slight bit of joy
That you like being at our house
Enough to cry a tear or two,
When it's time to leave.

Our fixing effort,
One we apply with the tear or two?
Well, of course, we tell you to
Make Mom and Dad
Bring you back soon!

Orange Push-Ups

When I see an Orange Push-up,
I think of you,
Of our hikes
To the town library,
Stopping along the way
To watch firemen in training
Or to explore the caboose parked
Alongside the tracks.

Best part, though,
Were walking trips home
When we'd stop by
Habersham Hardware,
Freezer by the
Front door, where you'd
Make your selection,
Always an Orange Push-up,
An orange stream to your elbows
By the time
We got home.

Cows

We know all about fabrics,
Can call them by name,
Wools and cottons and polyester blends.

We can name them tweeds or solids,
Checks or plaids,
Even whimsical prints.

But who knew
You had your own designation
Cows you would see.

The city girl coming to visit,
You called them as you saw them,
The polka-dotted cows.

Old Chair

No fancy art supplies
Necessary, not in your
Tiny hands.

A pencil, a crayon,
A coloring page, the back of a
Church bulletin.

They provide what's necessary,
For you, little Dali, Picasso,
Or Rembrandt.

Though at the time a bit of consternation
Arose about the permanent marker piece done on my
Old chair.

Heartbreak for Little Kids

Funny the things that spell
Heartbreak for little kids
Might be a break in a special toy,
Might be Mommy's leaving them
In the care of someone else,
Might be the suggestion
They go to bed when
It feels for certain the day
Just got started.

Heartbreak for you
Of a different sort,
We took you to
The restaurant, served
You your favorite food.
But a kid, on a kid's timetable,
Ate a bite, rested, talked,
With waitress assuming you'd finished.

But she—she was very wrong—
Both in assuming you'd finished,
But mostly in clearing your plate,
Without checking with you.

Luckily, she got an earful of it,
Not the spaghetti, but your angry words,
"I not finished!"

Hide-and-Seek

The bonus of being the pastor,
Was the short walk across the street,
To sprawling grounds with walking trails,
And the prized-by-all-children church playground,

It was there we spent time,
Whiling away the hours,
Spinning 'til dizzy on the merry-go-'round,
Climbing stairs to the top, then sliding down.

You begged, each of you,
For pushes higher and higher,
A contest in height
With the one seated next to you.

But especially I remember
Our games of hide-and-seek,
Older ones, more clued in
To the game's proceedings . . .

Would run distances away
As I hid my eyes,
But then there was Oscar,
Youngest at the time.

Every game, no matter
How many times, I'd finish
Counting, Oscar in plain sight,
Right under the slide.

I'd feign defeat
And call loudly, "Oscar, where are you?"
Your tiny voice rings today in my ears,
Same as if it were just yesterday…

MaMaw, here I am!

Good Luck to You

Wisely Mom and Dad
Thought through
possible mortification
for the teenager with boyfriend coming
to their door for the first time.

Knowing the infinite
possibilities of words
of embarrassment from the mouths
of the younger two, they hurry them off,
banish them upstairs.

Oh, Mom! Oh, Dad!
these little ones—
they're way ahead of you,
They find their way to the balcony
right over their own front door.

Introductions to Mom and Dad having been
accomplished and breathing a deep sigh of relief
they make their way to the car,
soon to be off and away from potential points
of embarrassment, from these, her younger siblings.

That's precisely the moment
they hear words
wafted from the balcony,
floating on air,
"Good luck, Maggie! Good luck to you!"

Reciprocate

It's a hard job,
But one assigned
You, that no one
Else can do
As can you.

When boyfriends
Show up at the door
Or when one's
On the phone
You never spare volume
For something wholly
Embarrassing to them,
Your older siblings.

But you—
You're the youngest two,
So what will happen,
Happen to you
When it's your turn
For dating,
All of them gone
And living lives
Of their own,
Who will reciprocate,
Reciprocate for you?

Picture Window

Some call them
Picture windows,
Those huge panes
Of glass, bedecking
Ranch-style homes
That many of us knew
As children.

They offered us
Views of streets
And cars and
Passengers all
Trying to get somewhere.

On this day,
There we were,
All of us
Standing front of
The picture window,
Watching as smiling dad
Bathed you—
Your very first bath,
Then presented you to us,
Ready to go somewhere
In the world.

Oh, the Joy

I held you on my lap,
Your little head near my knees,
Your bent legs barely touching my body,
And just that way,
We had oh so many
Meaningful conversations . . .
About what fun we would have together,
About the places we would go,
About parks, and playgrounds,
And swing sets and sandboxes,
And sometimes you cooed your response,
Other times you laughed out loud.

Oh, the joy of having you on my lap,
But, oh, the joy and the wonder
Of looking up as you tower over me!

Mother of Mary

Mother Mary, Mother of God,
You were there to the bitter end,
But where was your mother?
Had she died long ago,
Knowing too much already
Of bitterness, and anger, and rejection
Turned on the child she loved alongside of you?
Or was she there all along,
Simply discarded for lack of space
In the history of salvation?
Did she kneel with you
At the foot of the cross—
Worn-out knees and all—
To give you comfort while
Her heart was breaking too?
Did she take you home,
Insist you lie down,
Make you warm soup,
Hold you as you cried with never a tear
Of her own in your presence?

Oh, God of us all,
Surely you must have a special place in heaven
For mothers who nurture their children in love,
Surely you must have a soft spot in your heart
For grandmothers who love their children,
Love their children's children,
And watch, pillars of faith,
As the unimaginable unfolds
In their midst.

Salvation

Lines and crevices,
Aches and pains,
But more than these—
Failures and disappointments,
Betrayals and losses
Age us beyond mere years.

But in the presence of babies—
Especially as we hold our grandchildren—
Hope and promise.
Love and joy
Are born once again in us
And erase effects of years gone by.

Perhaps that is why
God came as a baby in a manger,
He came to be salvation—
For his grandparents, for grandparents through the ages.

www.ingramcontent.com/pod-product-compliance
Lightning Source LLC
Chambersburg PA
CBHW070455090426
42735CB00012B/2562